GW00480589

THE ANTI CHRIST

BY GEORGE W. CAREY

CONTENT

PART I.

Primitive Christians, the Essenes, fully realized and taught the great truth that Christ was a substance, an oil or ointment contained especially in the Spinal Cord, consequently in all parts of the body, as every nerve in the body is directly or indirectly connected with the wonderful "River that flows out of Eden (the upper brain) to water the garden."

The early Christians knew that the Scriptures, whether writ- ten in ancient Hebrew or the Greek, were allegories, parables or fables based on the human body "fearfully and wonderfully made."

These adepts knew that the secretion (gray matter—creative) that issues, (secretes) from the cerebrum, was the source and cause of the physical expression called man; and they knew that the "River of Jordan" was symbolized in the spinal cord and that the "Dead Sea" was used to symbolize the Sacred Plexus at the base of the spinal column where the Jordan (spinal cord) ends, typifying the entrance of Jordan into the Dead Sea.

The thick, oily and salty substance composing the Sacral Plexus, "Cauda Equina," (tail of the horse) may be likened unto crude Petroleum, (Petra, mineral, or salt, and oleum—Latin for oil) and the thinner substance, oil or ointment in spinal cord, may be compared with coal oil; and when this oil is carried up and crosses the Ida and Pingala (two fluid nerves that end in a cross in medulla oblongata where it contacts the cerebellum (Golgotha —the place of the skull) —this fluid is refined, as coal oil is refined, to produce gasoline—a higher rate of motion that causes the ascension of the airship.

When the oil (ointment) is crucified—(to crucify means to increase in power a thousand fold not to kill) it remains two days and a half, (the moon's period in a sign) in the tomb (cerebellum) and on the third day ascends to the Pineal Gland that connects the cerebellum with the Optic Thalmus, the Central Eye in the Throne of God that is the chamber overtopped by the hollow (hallowed) caused by the curve of the cerebrum (the "Most High" of the body) which is the "Temple of the Living God" the living, vital substance which is a precipitation of the "Breath of Life" breathed into man —therefore the "Holy (whole) Ghost" or breath.

The Pineal Gland is the "Pinnacle of the Temple." The modus operandi by which the oil of the spinal cord reaches the Pineal Gland is described in Part II.

PART II.

"There is no name under Heaven whereby ye may be saved except Jesus Christed and then crucified" (correct rendering of the Greek text).

Every twenty-eight and one-half days, when the moon is in the sign of the zodiac that the sun was in at the birth of the native, there is a seed or Psycho—Physical germ born in the or out of, the Solar Plexus (the Manger) and this seed is taken up by the nerves or branches of the Pneumo gastric nerve, and becomes the "Fruit of the Tree of Life," or the "Tree of good and evil"—viz : good if saved and "cast upon the waters" (circulation) to reach the Pineal Gland; and evil if eaten or consumed in sexual expression on physical plane, or by alcoholic drinks, or gluttony that causes ferment—acid and even alcohol in intestinam tract—thus—"No drunkard can inherit from the Kingdom of Heaven" *for acids and alcohol cut, or chemically split, the oil that unites with the mineral salts in the body and thus produces the monthly seed.*

This seed, having the odor of fish was called Jesus, from Ichtos, (Greek for fish) and Nun (Hebrew for fish) thus "Joshua the son of Nun," "I am the bread of life;" "I am the bread that came down from heaven;" "Give us this day our daily bread."

The fruit of the Tree of Life, therefore, is the "Fish-bread" of which thou shalt not eat on the plane of animal or Adam (earth-dust of the earth plane) : but to "Him that overcometh will I give to eat of the fruit of the Tree of Life" because he saved it and it returned to him in the cerebellum, the home of the Spiritual man, the Ego.

The cerebellum is heart shaped and called the heart in Greek—thus "As a man thinketh in his heart so is he." The bodily organ that men in their ignorance call heart is termed divider or pump in Greek and Hebrew. Our blood divider is not the button that we touch when we think, but it is the upper lobe of cerebellum that vibrates thought. The lower lobe is the animal (mortal) lobe that governs the animal world—that section of the body below the Solar Plexus, called lower Egypt—natural body—kingdom of earth—Appollyon—the Devil (lived, spelled backward) Satan (Saturn governs the bowels), etc.

Fire and Brimstone (the lake of fire) comes from the fact that sulphur (brimstone) is the prime factor in generating the rate of motion called heat, and overeating develops a surplus of sulphur.

The Seed, born every twenty-eight and one-half days, making 13 in 365 days, that is 13 months, remains two and one-half days in Bethlehem (house of bread), then is carried up Pneumo (or vagus) gastric nerve and across the medulla oblongata
and enters the cerebellum to remain two and one-half days, thus —"When Jesus was about twelve He appeared in the Temple teaching the doctors."

The age of puberty is about twelve. Then the first horn seed appears and the sensation caused by its vibration tempts the native on the lower plane to do the thing that slays it, which is fully explained in Genesis by the serpent—sex desire—tempting Adam and Eve (allegorical characters). From Krishna to Moses and Jesus serpents and Pharaohs and He-rods have striven to slay the first born.

From the age of twelve to thirty in the life of Jesus nothing is recorded, for twelve refers to puberty, and 30 or 3 means physical, mental and spiritual, viz: body, (flesh or soul) fluids and Spirit (the Ego).

Breath is translated "soul" over 500 times in the Bible, therefore soul is precipitated air (spirit) which may be lost in physical desire and expression (waste or sin, viz: to fall short) or saved by Regeneration. Read Matt. 17-28; also 1st Epistle of John 3-9. So, at the age of 30, Jesus, the seed, began to preach to body, soul and spirit, and as the seed was (or is) descending the spinal cord, the substance of which is symbolized by a formula of characters I. O. H. N. (as we symbolize water by H2O) it was baptized of John (no by John). Synonyms:— Saul, John, Christ, Or (gold). Jordan (word. Lord, oil, ointment).

Baptize is from the Greek Bapto, the effect of two chemicals when they unite and produce force that neither possessed singly. Here the seed, immersed in the oil, John, was so increased in power that "The Spirit of God descended like a dove and a voice out of Heaven said, 'This is my beloved son,' " etc.

Jordan means the descender—Dove, (to dive, a diver—see dictionary). Thus Jesus, the seed, was the son of man—the carpenter or builder until it was baptized in the precious ointment that was secreted from the Most High (brain) and descended the spinal cord and was thus given power to start on its journey to Jerusalem (God's City of Peace) and to be crucified at Place of Skull, then remain two and one-half days in the tomb, and on the third day ascend to the Father.

As this seed consumes its force every twenty-eight and one- half days and another (born first) comes out of the Solar Plexus (Bethlehem), we see why he was (is) a "Sacrifice for our sins"; also we see that, as this seed, taking on the Christ oil, is enabled to reach the pineal gland and cause it to vibrate at a rate that heals all manner of diseases—that the statement "The blood of Christ cleanseth from all sin" or deficiencies viz : falling short of substance is, literally true.

PART III.

During the first 300 years of the Christian era all that has been above written was understood by the real Christians, and about the end of that time the persecution of these Essenes by the priesthood became so marked that they met in secret and always made the sign of the fish.

About the year 325, Constantine, the pagan Roman Emperor, a monster in human form, like Nero, and the beast of August, 1914, called the degenerate teachers of Christianity together at Nicea.

Constantine murdered his mother and boiled his wife in oil because they still held to the original doctrines of the Essenes. Constantine was told by the Priests of his time that there was no forgiveness for crimes such as his, except through a long series of incarnations; but the anti-Christ sought to concoct a plan by which he hoped to cheat the Cosmic law.

And so it came to pass, after months of wrangling and fighting over the writings of the primitive Christians who clothed the wonders of the human body in oriental imagery, that the council, sometimes by a bare majority vote, decided which of the manuscripts were the "Word of God" and which were not.

The very important point in the minds of those ignorant priests—whether or no an angel had wings—was decided in favor of wings by three majority. The minority contended that, as Jacob let down a ladder for angels to descend and ascend upon it was prima facie evidence that angels do not have wings.

Just think, for a moment, upon the colossal ignorance of these priests who did not know that Jacob in Hebrew means "heel catcher" or circle, and that ladder referred to the influence of the signs of the zodiac upon the earth; and as one sign rising every two hours forms a circle every twenty-four hours (the four and twenty Elders of Revelation) the outer stars of the rising suns (sons) "catching on" to the last sons (suns) of the sign ascending. But now we come to the anti-Christ:

The council of Nicea, dominated by Constantine, voted that the symbols of the human body were persons; that Jesus was a certain historical man, a contention utterly and indubitably without foundation, in fact, and that all who believed (?) the story would be saved and forgiven here, and now. The idea appealed to the monster Constantine as an easy way out of his troubled mind and so the scheme of salvation by the actual blood of a real man or god was engrafted in the world.

Constantine and his dupes saw that the only way to perpetuate the infamy was to keep the world in ignorance of the operation of the Cosmic Law, so they changed "Times and seasons."

The date that they made the sun enter Aries was March 21st. Why? March 21st should be the first day of Aries, the head, April 19th should be the first day of Taurus, the neck, and so on through the twelve signs; but these designing schemers knew that by thus suppressing the truth the people might come to realize what was meant by "The heavens declare the glory of

God." Again: the moon, in its monthly round of 28½ days enters the outer stars (or suns) of a constellation two and one-half days before it enters the central suns of the constellations that are known as the Signs of the Zodiac or the "Circle of Beasts." But even unto this day the whole anti-Christ world (so-called "Christian") except the astrologers, go by almanacs that make the moon enter a sign of the zodiac two and one-half days before it does enter it and thus perpetuate the lie of the pagan Constantine, the anti-Christ.

Let me close with a deadly parallel:

ANTI-CHRIST	CHRIST
Christ was a man born of a woman. He died, and He will come again.	"Lo ! I am with you always." "He that believeth (believe means to do) SHALL never die."
We are Christians and expect to die and then be saved.	"The wages of sin is death." "All that I do ye can do." "Be ye therefore perfect even as your father is perfect."
Christ is greater than man, therefore can save us.	Know ye not that the Holy Ghost (breath) dwelleth in you?"
Only Jesus was conceived by the Holy Ghost.	"The Kingdom of Heaven is within you."
We must die in order to get into the "Kingdom." The earth will be destroyed.	"The earth endureth forever." "Thy will be done in earth as in heaven."
I am a Christian.	"These SIGNS shall follow those who believe in me : they shall lay hands on the sick and they shall recover."
I am born of God because I believe, or think, that a crucified saint, or good man, will save me from sin.	"He that is born of God will not sin for his seed remaineth in him."

For more evidence that Jesus and Christ are in your flesh see 1st Epistle of John—4th Chapter, 2nd and 3rd verses.

The Greek and Hebrew texts of our Scriptures plainly teach that Jesus and Christ, John and baptism, crucifixion and ascension, the triumph of the Ego over the "Enemy death" are in the substance and potentialities of the body; and that these fluids can and will save the physical body if conserved and not consumed (or wasted) in sexual or animal desire.

All of whatever name or religious denomination who teach a contrary doctrine agree with Constantine who appeared in the "Latter days" of the Pure Christian Practice.

Who is the anti-Christ? Look at a world of ruins. Does a good tree bring forth evil fruit?

The so-called teachers of, and believers in Christianity believe as Constantine and his priests, that Christ is "out in the desert" of the Judean hills—out on Calvary. Do they ever look for the meaning of Calvary in Greek? Calvary means a skull, and Golgotha—the place of the skull, exactly where the seed is crucified.

One-half of the combatants in the world's Armageddon have been praying, as Constantine prayed, "for God's help for Christ's sake." The other half pray to the same imaginary God and Christ out in "The desert" of their own ignorance for "peace and victory."

Return and come unto the God and Christ within you, oh! ye deluded ones, and the bugles will all sing truce along the iron front of war and the "Ransomed of the Lord will return to Zion with songs and everlasting joy upon their faces."

Printed in Great Britain
by Amazon

23219182R10015